For the Love of Mike

An Inspirational Race For Life

By

Jean Overdorf Thornton

For the Love of Mike

For information address:

SHADYBROOK PUBLISHING
c/o 1429 Chase Court
Carmel, Indiana 46032
Phone 317-844-8622

ISBN: 0-9634373-5-6

Second Printing 2003

Cover design by Brandon Corbin

Printed on recycled paper.

Acknowledgments

My sincere thanks to all my family for their steadfast support and confidence; to my daughters, Linda Foster and Susan Wall; to my husband Garnet for his help which freed me to write; to my two immutable supporters, Fern O. Sweet, my sister, and Darlene Overdorf. Special thanks to my son, Bob Thornton, who has encouraged me through many difficult and painful days of remembering and writing.

I thank Mike's parents, Steve and Chloie Cowan, and his sister, Elisa Fox for their help and support. Thanks to Joy Scott Forsman for her editing skills. Thanks also to my great-niece Nancy Overdorf Cline who has read my manuscripts as they have progressed and is my primary cheering section!

To Bill Corbin and his staff, whose enthusiasm, care and personal attention to every minute detail of the publishing of this book could not have been surpassed, I thank you from the bottom of my heart!

Especially I say thanks to all of the dedicated doctors, nurses, and caregivers who cared for Mike: to Dr. Arthur Provisor and Dr. Dan McMahon of Riley Hospital for Children in Indianapolis. Thanks to Dr. Michael E. Trigg who performed Mike's bone marrow transplant at the University *of Iowa Hospital and was Mike's captain as well as "co-partner" each step of the way in the final battle to save his life.*

Thanks also to Kevin Sauer, the former rowing coach at Purdue University, presently at the University of Virginia, and his wife Barbara, who gave Mike the hope of attaining a scholarship when all hope seemed to have deserted him; to Ross Dwiggins, Mike's coach at Kokomo High School, and Dr. Bill Madauss, both of whose encouragement influenced me to publish this book when I was wavering; to Chuck Jansen for many pictures and articles; to Jeff Dwiggins for his tribute to Mike, portions of which have been edited into the completed manuscript; and to all of you who have "been there" for Mike, and for me, all along.

I am especially grateful for the permission of all the above named medical personnel to use their names. None of them requested to read the drafts nor required that they approve any portion of the manuscript before publication of this book. I sincerely thank each of them for their confidence in me and assure them it is highly valued.

Foremost and above all, I am grateful to the omnipotent Father of us all Who was always there, and here, each step of the way...from the beginning to the end...and beyond...even forever.

Foreword

The opinions and descriptions in this book are strictly those of the author. I am not in the medical field and make no claim to medical knowledge other than the mere basics. This is not about medical knowledge, nor the lack of it.

It is simply an account of one courageous young man's experiences through the devastating illness called "leukemia," compiled and written by a member of his family who loved him. However, this book could never have been written without also including the same astonishing and prevalent courage, optimism, acceptance and great gusto for life encountered in all of the children and young people who crossed the pages of this book. Crossing paths with each of them was a privilege and inspiration beyond belief until experienced! May it be the same for you.

For any medical terminology or report errors, I humbly ask the reader's indulgence.

For the Love of Mike

"Trailing clouds of glory do we come... from God Who is our home..."

(From "Intimations of Immortality" by Wordsworth)

Introduction

February 1988

As I sit here on this salt-and-sand-bleached dock at Clearwater Beach, Florida, and look across the Bay, I remember a boy named "Mike." Fifteen year old athlete Michael Scott Cowan, who stole my heart and mind...one who kept notes, and asked me to do likewise, through a devastating terminal illness so that he might one day write a book to let other kids know that they, too, like him, could be a winner in life even though they might be stricken with a terrible disease called leukemia. Well, he never got the book written, but I have his notes as well as mine, and so I will write this book for him because it was important to him...because it must be written. Mike most certainly was a winner in every endeavor he undertook, including leukemia. And so this book is written totally "for the love of Mike." Remember that although it tells of many trying and sad occasions, the overall message of this book is one of courage, hope and joy...all about life...glorious life, and winning...winning in attitude, faith and love. To quote from Mike: *"Never Give Up!"*

"NEVER GIVE UP!"

"NEVER GIVE UP!!"

For the Love of Mike

Chapter One

The muffled sounds of the rhythmic pounding of four pairs of Nike-clad feet slowed and then subsided as the silent runners appeared at the turn of the long hall, abruptly coming to a halt on the highly polished floor. As suddenly as the sterile quiet of the hospital corridor had been broken by the approach of the teen-aged athletes— Pat Pollard, Jeff Dwiggins, Tom Kirkmeyer, and Kevin Renie— once again it had been restored. They had rerouted their practice run that March morning in 1985 to go past the Kokomo, Indiana, St. Joseph Hospital. Now they were silently approaching the room where the fifth member of their 1984-85 cross-country high school track team was undergoing tests to determine the cause of his tiredness and unaccustomed lethargy and lack of enthusiasm.

"Acute Myologonous Leukemia; Mike, I am sorry." The words spoken only moments earlier by the concerned doctor were like a judge's death sentence...incomprehensible words suspended in the air like a fragile spider's web. The athletes surged into the room...the runners surrounding one

1

of their own, their arms encircling him and each other. As they squatted and huddled together around their friend sitting on the side of the bed with his head in his hands, their hushed voices and choked sobs soon filled the room.

My mind flashed back a short fifteen-and-a half-years earlier to the maternity ward in the same hospital. Dr. Schwartz, the family's doctor, walked out of the delivery room carrying a squirming newborn, still unwashed baby boy in a receiving blanket and holding him out to me, said. "I thought you'd like to meet your new grandson." "Oh, I'm not his grandmother...I'm only his aunt, his great-aunt." As he handed him to me, the doctor replied, "That's OK, you'll do." And thus, Mike and I met...and bonded!

Earlier that day, I had brought his mother to the hospital delivery room as his father was at work. Several years earlier my husband and I had been appointed legal guardians of the little eight year old girl who lived with her grandparents in the country around the corner from us, and who would one day become Mike's mother. It seemed only natural that it was I who took her to the hospital that day, and that later the entire family came to our home for a few days so that we all might care for the newborn and his mother. Both Mike's father and my husband worked in Kokomo, so that worked out fine. And so it was that it was to "Aunt Jean and Uncle Garnet's house" that Mike went from Kokomo St. Joseph Hospital in November of 1969, A. D., and again on the 13th March of 1985, A.C.D. (After Cancer Diagnosis).

The intervening years were so eventful for the bright

and lovable little boy, who had inherited from his maternal grandfather, a merchant marine from Oslo, Norway, his blond hair and light coloring. When he was not quite four years old, his little sister, Elisa, was born. Though the family unit was temporarily separated due to health problems of his mother, there was always much love and closeness in the family. Mike's dad tenderly and lovingly cared for his two children while holding down a job in a factory, and still faithfully saw to it that each weekend his little family was reunited at the hospital where the mother was being treated over a period of time.

In spite of the stress in his life, Mike blossomed. He was an exceptional child with his wheat colored hair, clear blue eyes, and the disposition of the sunshine—and always an achiever in every endeavor he undertook. As Mike grew older, he became more confident, motivated and competitive, yet was neither selfish nor arrogant even though the awards and ribbons continued to mount in number. Not a vocal leader, he lead by example...a natural motivational leader, always encouraging his teammates (as well as himself) to strive for perfection in the sports that he loved so much. His coach explained it to me in these words, "Mike has the inner drive you wish all your kids had." Always the peacemaker at school as well as at home—almost like an angel unaware.

The entire family was proud of him...we all accepted his unselfish and thoughtful ways largely for granted. He was just Mike and that was the way he was and had always been! From day one there existed a special and mutual bond between Mike and me. It was fun (for both of us) to help him fix a bulletin board to display his mounting ribbons and awards. At the holidays, it was such a joy to fix him, as well as all the other members of our family, the special foods so anticipated and enjoyed. At the top of Mike's list were homemade noodles with chicken, and a close second was the buttered corn. Not the usual sweets and traditional "junk food," but the noodles with mashed potatoes, and succulent sweet corn. Corn that had been grown on the farm, quickly harvested and frozen, until it was gently cooked and served. When prepared this way, it was impossible to tell from the fresh corn collected on a hot summer day right from the field. These were the favorites...and they were always on the menu for both Thanksgiving and Christmas when all of our families gathered together each year for the holidays.

Chapter Two

February, 1989...on the dock in Florida...

*T*here was no warning of the impending cloud of cancer that struck so unexpectedly that March of 1985. Mike had achieved a perfect attendance record for three years at his school; he rarely had any illness other than a brief cold. His was not a rowdy disposition; he just "blended" and never raised waves. Still the devilish glint in his eye and the quick wit made one very aware of his presence. What he possessed was a natural sincerity and genuineness that could never be pretended or put-on. (Perhaps the best word to describe Mike would be character—character which never went unrecognized by his teachers nor family, and especially not by his peers.)

Mike's father, a Vietnam veteran, had been laid-off temporarily from the factory where he worked, and as the long months passed the family insurance policy had expired and soon the unemployment checks also would cease.

The baffling flu-like symptoms that Mike could not throw off that February were largely ignored by him...a doctor bill would definitely be another financial burden and anyway he was young and strong; he would get well on his own.

Mr. Dwiggins, Mike's coach, was baffled. If he hadn't known Mike better, he would have been certain that somehow the boy had lost his drive...his positive will to exceed and win. Finally he called him in to his office and explained that even though he (Mike) had come in great in the state in his group of freshmen runners in 1984, he could not rest on his laurels. In short, to "shape up!" Mike agreed and started the run the following day only to have to stop and, while vomiting, admit to himself and others, that he was feeling bad, very bad. But now it would be OK to go check on it, because the family's insurance was once again reinstated as his father had thankfully been recalled to work.

The call to me from his mother informed us that the blood cell count was such that the doctor suspected mononucleosis, but if it weren't that, they would also test for more serious causes...hepatitis, or possibly leukemia. We quickly reassured each other that it had to be something simple because Mike was so healthy and strong...had almost never been sick. And so I had gone to the hospital where the tests were being performed to be with the family as we awaited the results. As the assorted grandmothers, parents, cousins, aunts and uncles all waited in his hospital room, we all were still reassuring each other that it would (must) be "mono." Mike had always been the epitome of health, had not even had the "I feel too sick to go to school—my stomach aches" syndrome of the very young, we kept reassuring each other, and ourselves. No headaches, no temper tantrums, no complaints—just always eager and ready to go, to compete and excel, the original positive thinker and motivator, the leader, psychologically, of his teammates with his never-failing—we can and we will! The bulletin board filled with ribbons, at home in his room, confirmed his attitude—he could and he did!

There surely can be nothing more immobilizing, more paralyzing with fear, more painful to hear than the diagnosis: Cancer…Leukemia… particularly to an innocent child—a young person who has not yet lived, to start the long and torturous road to an unknown destination. The emotions felt in that room encompassed shock, disbelief, unbelievable heartache, and fear, and yes, anger. Why? Why? WHY?

As the doctor said those fateful words, Mike who was standing in the middle of the hospital room—Mike, the picture of the all American fifteen-year-old boy: handsome, tall and well built, straight as an arrow, clear blue eyes, thick hair the color of ripe wheat, a firm chin—Mike held out his hand to the doctor he had known most of his life and as they shook hands, in a voice that barely wavered, the youth softly said, "Thank you." As God is my witness, those were the exact words spoken. He knew the sadness the doctor was feeling at the disclosure and felt compassion for him. That was Mike, personified.

The doctor turned and left the room and as I followed and called to him, he turned and I saw the tears in his eyes. Shortly we heard the approaching runners as Mike's teammates arrived. The strong athletic team had never achieved more perfect timing than when they entered the room only moments after Mike had slumped down prone on his bed holding his head in his hands, the facts of the doctor's words penetrating his mind and soul, as the tears came.

The first night passed like an unreal mirage. Mike and I went to the Ponderosa steak house just across the street from the hospital. My husband and I had promised the whole family a T-bone dinner (Mike's favorite) as soon as we heard the "verdict" and could celebrate a flu or even a mono diagnosis. Even then, we religiously practiced positive thinking.

Everybody but Mike and I declined, and while the rest, stunned with the report, went on over to Mike's home, we still went across to the Ponderosa. In the restaurant that night was the first really revealing talk that Mike and I shared. After a couple of disinterested bites, he pushed his food aside and thoughtfully and painstakingly lay bare his thoughts. "My main worry is Elisa," he began. "I'm worried this will keep me from getting my college scholarship. After I got that, I could easy put her through college. Aunt Jean, she is so smart and works so hard in school, she deserves to go to college." And I wholeheartedly agreed with him as Elisa, his 12½ year old sister also was very competitive and bright. "Don't worry about that, Mike, Elisa will have the opportunity to go to college. Our energy and concern now is to get you well, OK?" "OK..." And then the anguished question came, "Why me, Aunt Jean, why me? I have never smoked...I have never even tried "pot" once; why I haven't even ever drank a beer! What have I done that I've got leukemia? WHY ME?" (Why, indeed? Maybe because of the rigid training and discipline all runners adhered to—at times running until they literally collapsed in exhaustion? The Agent Orange that his father was exposed to during his time in Vietnam? The inordinate amount of stress that Mike had known in his young life?) All of these were questions we could not answer.

The questions were buzzing through both our heads equally. "Mike, let's resolve today to use two mottoes until that day comes when you are all well. First: to take One Day at a Time, and secondly (not necessarily in that order) to use the Serenity Prayer as our guide. "Dear Heavenly Father, grant me the serenity to accept the things I cannot change, the courage to change the things I can, and the wisdom to know the difference. Amen." We agreed those would be our guide and our strength. And they were.

Finally we went to his home and picked up his mother and they spent the night at our house. The next morning his dad picked us up to go on to Riley Hospital in Indianapolis, a distance of slightly more than 50 miles from Mike's home in Kokomo. (A trip they would drive almost daily for months to come.) The doctor had warned me in the hall to watch for any bleeding that night before we took him on to

9

Riley Hospital the next morning. "Where?" "Anywhere…the nose, ears, eyes, rectum…anywhere." Dear God, what is this leukemia?

After a sleepless night—how do you check a sleeping (?) 15-year-old boy for bleeding when he has gone into his room and very politely, but firmly, closed the door? That's right, I didn't. He needed his time, his pride, and his privacy; and as I heard the typical teenage music playing on his radio, I gave a silent little prayer of thanks. Even if it was only to drown the sounds of the tears, he had not retreated into a silent shell of his own making. He was bright; he would call his mother or me if there were any blood in the urine or stool…or on his pillow. He would overcome this leukemia. We would lick it! The hours dragged by until dawn.

Chapter Three

Ward "B" at the James Whitcomb Riley Hospital for Children in Indianapolis was located in the basement of the very old building. It smelled of antiseptics, children's toys and crayons, and dog-eared storybooks...and frequently of less than freshly bathed bodies as many parents brought their children there as outpatients—plus all of those who were resident patients. It encompassed a very large area that always seemed full-to-overflowing with patients in the tiny cubicle examining rooms where the doors were usually left open...very possibly for better ventilation.

As we passed one of the rooms while proceeding from one area to the next with Mike that morning, I heard an infant's "new-born" sounding cries. Looking in the direction of the wails, I saw a tiny baby boy receiving a spinal tap examination. In addition to the spinal contraption, there were tubes from the top of his head as well as from one tiny foot. I recoiled in horror, making sure to make no comment, nor hearing one. Reading the obituaries a short time later, I learned that the baby was the three-week-old son of one of the physicians on the staff right there at Riley. So leukemia does not play favorites!

Seated in one of the rocking chairs was a fashionably dressed young mother reading a novel...seemingly oblivious to the child seated in a small chair close to her. About five years old with a face that was so swollen and round, the features were nearly stretched flat, the sad little eyes expressionless. Without the beautiful little ruffled pink and white flowered pajamas and matching robe that she wore, one would never have known if she were a girl or boy with her shiny hairless little head. The child did not seem aware of her mother's presence, either, and I could not understand the seeming indifference of the mother who read while ignoring her child so completely.

Even as I was pondering how I could approach the oblivious mother to see if I might read to the little girl, Mike's name was called and we proceeded into Dr. Provisor's office for his first consultation. However, a few weeks later I got acquainted with the little girl's mother and learned the story of her apparent "uncaring attitude." The child was the last of her three children. She had already lost her other two to the same disease that was now claiming the life of her third and last child! A one in a million chance and it had happened to her, and her ways of coping were to lose herself in her novels! How sad for her...as well as for her child. She had found the shell of non-existence in the real world, as I would find so many of them did later, in books, crossword puzzles, and sitting as far away as possible from the patients in the corners of their rooms.

Mike's two primary physicians were Dr. Arthur Provisor and Dr. Dan McMahon, who quickly confirmed the former diagnosis. Upon meeting them, I was struck with the total contrast in their personalities and appearance. A true study in contrast...Dr. Provisor, tall, thin, noisy, boisterous, brash, blunt, loving, sports minded (which delighted Mike who loved to discuss any and all of the teams, high school, college, and professional) and Jewish. A father, Dr. Provisor was married to a pediatrician in private practice. And then there was Dr. McMahon...shorter, well built, soft spoken, reserved, quiet, brilliant, his conversation very thought out, Catholic, and like his colleague, a solid family man. Both of the men, however, with all of their differences, were identical in two respects...their complete dedication to their all too often hopeless tasks, and their unswerving love and devotion to their "kids."

They were alike, also, in their totally honest, and sometimes almost brutally frank, discussions with both the patients and their families. Mike immediately hit it off with Dr. Provisor who said upon completing his initial examination, "Well, Mike, my plans are for you to be bringing in the awards with your running; I don't know what your plans are!" How wonderful it was to see the old familiar twinkle in Mike's eyes as he answered, "That's my plans, too."

Soon after checking in to his room in the Teen Unit at Riley Hospital, named for the famous Hoosier poet James Whitcomb Riley, the half-opened door was thudded soundly.

It suddenly "bounced" wide open to accommodate a bald headed, plump girl pushing, with total abandonment, a cumbersome steel apparatus on wheels. (The girl looked familiar. She had been one of three teens racing wheelchairs down the hall the first time we had entered the Teen Unit. The three were careening to cheers of encouragement from the other less active patients watching from their rooms. The racers passed these patient rooms as they made the oval around the center rooms that contained the nurse's station, kitchen, and combination cafeteria/school/recreation room. The nurses were skillfully sidestepping to avoid a collision, seemingly oblivious to all the commotion. That was the only race we witnessed, but it surely was a lively one!)

Suspended from the top of the steel cart were various bottles of medication and nutrition connected by a bevy of tubes to one of the girls' arms. With her other arm she was pushing the awkward contraption. The wheels were banging and clanging against first one object and then another, including both sides of the door, then against the dresser finally coming to a halt as it banged loudly and solidly against Mike's metal bed. The rooms were not all that large and held in addition to all the medical gear, all the stuff that every teenager "must have."

"Hi, I'm Sandy...what's your name? Mike? What's wrong with you? Oh, you got A.M.L. mine's A.L.L. Hey, don't let 'em scare you with all of this sh— stuff; it's not so bad if you don't let it scare you out. Boy, you sure look good with hair; I've got a wig, but I don't wear it; I hate the thing; my hair's blonde, too." A self-conscious laugh…"I mean my hair was blonde…it may come in green all the crap they keep giving me. You got any brothers or sisters? I had a brother five years older'n me, but he committed suicide when he knew I had cancer. My Dad and Mom got a divorce, too; well, it wasn't my real dad, but I called him my dad 'cause I don't know where my real one's at. How old are you? I'm 15. I'm in remission now. If they can find me a match, I hope I can get a BMT, (bone marrow transplant). Ain't that the life for you…my brother might have been the perfect match and he had to go kill hisself when he heard about me. Oh, well, catch you later, Mike…I gotta go catch the other two new kids that came in today. Hang loose, Mike, ya hear? See ya roun'."

As she charged out of the room exactly as she had entered, completely oblivious and uncaring of all the commotion and chaos she was creating, Mike's and my eyes met and held and simultaneously, as we heard her bumping and thumping her way far enough away to be out of hearing distance, we both dissolved in laughter. Wonderful, tension relieving, hysterical laughter. The only three words that Mike had uttered the entire time she stood there were "AML," "Mike," and "fifteen," and we laughed until tears rolled down our cheeks.

Mike seemed a little less depressed as he prepared a short time later for the young nurse who would assist in shampooing his cherished, stylishly mid-length and well-groomed hair. We decided to select a wig right away to match his natural color and texture as nearly as possible. Unfortunately, the ordered wig, in spite of the supposed "matching," was much darker than Mike's natural wheat-colored hair and he hated it with a passion. Once the rounds of chemotherapy were started, which was that same night, the hair would soon be a thing of the past. Remembering the visit from Sandy a short time before, once again the tension was broken by laughter, but maybe this time, the tears were all not from laughing too hard.

Chapter Four

February, 1990...
on the dock in Florida...continued

*A*s Mike's days of chemotherapy passed into weeks that spring of 1985, the remission we had prayed for did not materialize. His spirits never failed to rise with each new day, however, and with Sandy's dismissal upon having reached remission, Mike quickly became the ambassador of good will...the unofficial greeter and "cheerer-upper" as she had done on the day he arrived. Quickly we learned to distinguish the different kids in the Teen Ward.

There was Jim, short, energetic, the teen-unit's unofficial intellectual...a year older than Mike. Having survived one and a half year of A.L.L., he was the self appointed authority. His knowledge of all the treatments, the tests, the names of all the lethal, life saving chemicals was awesome. He loved to discuss at great length with Mike and each new patient, or their adult relatives, the merit and the disadvantages of the treatments as well as the options. The tongue twisting names of the drugs rolled off his tongue with the ease of a two-year-olds' "No." He also had a very positive attitude, due in part to his having beaten the deadly leukemia for so long a time.

Fifteen year old Peggy had already beaten insurmountable odds. After removing a cancer close to her kidney when she was five years of age, the wonderful doctor, knowing that the then unknown know-how and technology on the procedure to reconnect the different organs was imminent, had left parts intact that were normally removed when he placed the "bag" outside her abdomen 10 years earlier. What a glorious day to sit with her family in the surgical waiting room for the more than seven hours, when the surgeon walked out and with an almost ethereal glow of elation on his exhausted face declared, "It is finished; I am sure it is going to work!" Sometimes the tears that are shed at Riley Hospital for Children are tears of joy! For several days the joy over each time that Peggy successfully urinated naturally, was shared with the ecstatic parents, by many of us who had waited for the good news.

Joe, the largest boy in the Ward, probably idolized Mike most of all. Joe was at least 6'1", a 170-lb. high school junior. On the outside, his speech indicated a very self assured, handsome young man. Under the exterior bravado that appeared very mature, was a very frightened and insecure child. He wanted most of all to possess the unfeigned courage that Mike wore so naturally—natural because that was the way Mike really was.

For the Love of Mike

In Mike's third week at Riley, a new roommate arrived. Slender of build, dark curly hair, with skin that was very pale, almost translucent looking, Kevin had been diagnosed with AML four days earlier. Turning his head to the wall in the bed where he lay, his eyes vacant or closed to shut out reality, he ignored everyone including Mike. Having not eaten anything for the entire four days, they were threatening to start feeding him intravenously to avoid dehydration if he didn't start eating...and that soon! His mother's pleas fell on deaf ears...likewise, the scoldings. No rudeness...just no response at all.

Mike loved pizza which we were permitted to go pick up for him at a nearby Noble Roman's pizza shop. Equally loved were the pizza bread sticks with different dips—salsa, cheese, etc. Usually my husband or Mike's parents would pick up a few extras...they never went begging with so many teen-agers around. (Mike's parents and Elisa shared the delivery tasks with us to keep pizza available when they were requested, as we planned our visits to Mike so that one of us was always there a major part of each day until late in the evening. Of course, any time that Mike was able and permitted to leave, his parents and Elisa and he would go to Red Lobster for shrimp or some of the other favored area restaurants, or his uncle and I would take him to the MCL cafeteria at the nearby mall for fried chicken etc. It was a more than welcome break for all of us to get away from the hospital. However, never once did I hear him complain about the hospital. Once again, he was typically Mike and made the best of his lot.)

As the fragrant aroma of the warm breadsticks drifted from the bag with the assorted dips, Mike's first comment was, "Hey, Kevin, try one of these while they're hot. They sure beat the hospital food we've been eating," (totally ignoring the fact of the non-eating, of which he was fully aware). "Aunt Jean, take a couple over and some of this taco cheese dip, too, while they're piping hot. And how about a coke for you too, Kevin, when I order mine?" Quietly I sat in the chair of that small room while two hungry 15-year-old boys devoured 6 breadsticks, generously coated with taco cheese dip and two large cokes, their young laughter more beautiful than Tchaikovsky's most beautiful music.

A grateful mother's eyes brimmed with tears, as she wisely remained silent. It would be nice to say that Kevin's attitude changed and he became less reclusive, but that was not the case. He admitted defeat and surrendered when the enemy first attacked him, and the length of the battle was much shortened over those who resisted not only with their body through medications and nourishment, but perhaps more importantly with their will and spirit, through their mind. In his book *Man's Search for Meaning*, the famous Viennese psychologist Viktor Frankl showed that those who survived in the concentration camps were those who retained some degree of control, even in the most trivial things they did or even thought each day of their survival. Those who died first were those who had "given up" or surrendered mentally as well as physically.

For the Love of Mike

Sweet Tracy with long blonde hair seemed almost like a guardian angel. Having been in remission for more than a year, her beautiful hair bounced from side to side as she visited all the kids in the Teen Unit up and down the hall each time she came in for her check-ups, which were frequent. Being an only surviving child, her parents busy in the flower business, the kids she had come to know and love were her extended family and she always came laden with fresh flowers and plants. The pretty flowers she would deliver to the different rooms gave a special meaning to the term flower child. She truly was, in the highest sense, a beautiful and innocent "flower child."

If there was a special angel for Mike as he endured the hours of misery and pain, it had to be Abby, his special nurse. Abby—red headed, shy, gentle, caring, kind—she and Mike were almost like soul mates from the first moment the clear blue eyes met the amber-flecked brown ones. The petite 26-year-old single nurse and the blond old-beyond-his-years, teenager that towered over her met, and Mike's world became larger. She was his special nurse in every way; it was she who was there late at night when the chemo had made him feel so nauseous; it was she who comforted him when his courage would begin to falter; and it was she who would help to restore the positive attitude that was such an innate part of him. It was she who was there late at night when the tears were muffled in the pillow, and while pretending to not being aware of the tears, she would ask him if he were up to a game of scrabble. It was she who, realizing how much he depended on her in those late night and early morning hours, gave him her home phone number so that he could call her if she weren't on duty. It was she who visited us at our home on his "furloughs" later at Christmas, and again at New Year's Eve. It was she whose eyes meeting his made him aware of his manhood and her femininity; and yes, it was she who stirred the first serious love in Mike.

Mike was very popular and certainly had his share of girls whom he liked and frequently talked with on the phone there in the hospital, but this was on a completely different level. His lethal illness had matured him in every psychological way, as his disciplined athletic training had matured him physically, and it was Abby who had made the unbearable bearable. He adored her, and in a way perhaps we are not meant to understand, I firmly believe that love was reciprocated. Who could not love him? And who would not love this lovely angel of mercy?

Mike became very informed about every aspect of his disease, and of his impending bone marrow transplant (if he maintained remission from the disease and found a suitable donor.) Since he did not want his mother and dad to worry about the inherent dangers of the disease, he would read the brochures and detailed informative medical books and pass them on to me, all the while keeping the information he was collecting to himself. And asking me to do likewise. Those were his wishes, and so I did not question it. I understood that the ordeal ahead of him did not loom as quite so overwhelming if he could protect his parents and sister as long as possible and one of his main concerns was to spare his beloved family as much heartache as possible. Being the sensitive boy that he was, he was very aware of the pain that all of us who loved him were also having to bear, and he particularly wanted to protect his parents and sister in any way that he could.

As Mike became more informed about all of the aspects of his disease, I, too, was learning much along with him. We learned that leukemia is actually another name for cancer of the blood; that each person's blood is produced within the "bone marrow." There are two acute kinds...Acute Lymphocytic Leukemia, which usually strikes children, and the more serious Acute Myologenous Leukemia, the type that generally targets adults, but sometimes, as in Mike's case, it also can strike younger persons.

There are also Chronic types of both of the above, but these were not diagnosed in any of the children I met at Riley Hospital, and seem to usually affect adults or older adults. When the leukemia attacks and destroys the bone marrow, the only way, to date, to fight it is to first destroy the patient's bone marrow completely by chemotherapy, radiology etc. Of course, this process "kills" the leukemia, but in its total destruction, it also leaves the patient totally vulnerable...no immunity to anything!

If a 100% "match" can be found, which is rare except in either a twin or sometimes in a full sibling, a specified amount of bone marrow is extracted from the donor, and transferred through a tube directly into the vein of the patient. Actually it is just a moderate amount of the bone marrow that is extracted or required, because hopefully, it is then "accepted" by the one receiving it, without the body recognizing it as foreign and thus rejecting it. If this happens, the adopted marrow will then begin producing more healthy blood on its own. The closer the marrow match of the two persons involved, the greater the chances of a successful bone marrow transplant. The chance of a "perfect" match, other than either a brother or sister, is very slim indeed! Something like one in twenty thousand! We were praying for either Elisa's bone marrow to match Mike's, or a miracle!

One day after Mike had enjoyed playing with his younger cousins who had visited that day (my grandchildren), he became very serious. He said that he had read that the treatments he was receiving could render him sterile, and he was very worried about it. He told me how much that he had enjoyed Matt (5) and Emily (1) being there, and also Christopher (10) and Jennifer, my 12-year-old granddaughter who frequently came and drew caricatures and horses on the blackboard in his room. He continued that he loved kids and hoped someday to have a family of his own. However, he added, that in the medical book he was reading it told that a cancer patient's sperm could be harvested, frozen and stored for years if necessary, if it were done before it was destroyed from the effects of the chemotherapy used for cancer. He asked me if I would help him find out as soon as possible the needed additional information.

I agreed that I, too, hoped he would someday know the joy of having his own children (what wonderful character and qualities he possessed for that hoped-for possibility!) and I would find out if this could be done for him, which in fact, I did almost immediately. However, when one of the doctors told me that it was already too late for Mike, I decided that unless he mentioned it again to me, we would cross that bridge later down the road. (One day at a time.) He never brought up the subject again, nor did I.

Neither of the parents or Elisa's bone marrow was an exact match. Thus it was that the doctors were attempting, through their national computer hook-up with hospitals all over the United States, to find that one in 20,000 chance of a perfect match which would statistically give Mike a 20% chance of a successful BMT. It was a major decision, and yet without the BMT, his chances were practically nil.

As the decision was being discussed, one day when Dr. McMahon was waiting beside me for the down elevator, I asked his opinion...but before he could answer, I reworded the question. "If Mike were your son, what would you do? Would you want him to have the BMT?" After a long thoughtful pause he replied, "I would do it", and once again I saw tears of emotion in the eyes of the physician, the loving father of five children, who answered me. The choices and options weren't really all that numerous...20% chance with the bone marrow transplant, 0% without.

For the Love of Mike

Chapter Five

I n November of 1985, Mike had two important occasions to celebrate…he was in remission (even though it was a shaky one)…and he would celebrate his 16th birthday! He was once again at our house where he came nearly every time he was furloughed from Riley. There was more than one reason for this. He was very popular and well liked by most everyone. He loved going home to Kokomo where he could see and get together with all his friends. However, following all of the chemotherapy he had received, he was also very susceptible to colds or any of the other "bugs" that are commonly passed from one student to the next in schools. Of course, there would have been a steady stream of kids if he were at home in Kokomo (exactly as he would have wanted it to be!)

On one of those times when he was well enough to go home to Kokomo, and was given permission to do what he felt capable of doing, he was delighted to actually run with his teammates. That was without a doubt one of Mike's happiest days. On another occasion, he went to King's

Island, an amusement park in Cincinnati, Ohio, with Jeff Dwiggins, the friend that was most like a brother to Mike, and that was the epitome of pure unadulterated fun for both of them!

Though he loved seeing all his friends, his resistance was very low due to all the powerful drugs and chemicals used to get and keep the leukemia in remission, and most of the time it was safer for him to not be exposed to the diseases so prevalent in schools. It was a precaution that our home in the country helped to facilitate. The telephone has to be one of the biggest blessings of the 20th century. Mike heard from many of his friends at Kokomo, both boys and girls, and of course there was a special girl whose calls really brightened his days.

In addition, Mike loved having a large room that was all "his." The room had been vacated by our three kids as they had, one by one, left home when they went away to school. Mike had his own radio and television, and most important of all, he had his own space, telephone and privacy whenever he felt like it…by simply closing the door. And whenever he wanted to talk, the door was opened and the words were spoken, "Can we talk, Aunt Jean?" And of course, we always could…or play scrabble, his favorite game and certainly one of mine, too. He was fiercely competitive, as also was I, and he was good! Sometimes we would purposely make up long authentic sounding, but nevertheless phony words and let them "pass" just for the hilarious fun we had with them. Elisa was also a strong and very

astute competitor, but he warned me that she would sometimes cheat if he didn't watch her, and again we laughed as
I asked him whoever had taught her so well! Those were
really precious times for all of us. Mike's family had always
loved to play all sorts of games together.

Mike's birthday celebration was so special. His family was all at our house...his mother and dad and Elisa as
well as his grandmother. I had made a call to Bob Gregory,
the good-hearted weatherman on TV Channel 13, and had
explained that Mike was home from Riley awaiting a tenta-
tive BMT, and what a special young person he was. Mike's
eyes lit up with joy and surprise when his name was an-
nounced on the television show that night!

There were gifts and a birthday cake with candles
and the absolute indispensable "chicken and noodles" plus
all the trimmings. (All throughout Mike's eight months of
deep nausea and lack of appetite, the homemade noodles
with chicken were placed in pint (or quarts for sharing!)
size jars, taken to the hospital in a frozen state and kept in
the teen unit freezer. When desired, they could be thawed
and heated in the unit's microwave oven, and served at any
hour of the day or night...and frequently they were eaten at
very odd hours. They seemed to be the one food that Mike
could tolerate throughout the entire illness, and there were
always some available.) Of course, there was also the usual
happy teasing and bantering between him and his sister,
Elisa, and lots of pictures taken plus the singing of the happy
birthday song. Happiness abounded for those few hours

and things seemed almost normal.

Sometime, long after everyone had gone home and I had just gone to bed, there was a light knock at my bedroom door, and I heard Mike softly ask me if I was asleep, and if we could talk. I grabbed a robe and we went into his room. Looking at him, I knew something was troubling him deeply and waited as he looked down as he planned his words carefully. "Aunt Jean, would you do a favor for me?" As I nodded my head, he continued, "Now, don't think I am not thinking positive, because I believe I am going to come through all of this fine...but just in case something happens, there are two things I would like you to do." After a pause, he continued: "First of all, if I am on life support and I can't make it, will you see to it that I am taken off it...and second, if something happens, will you ask that people give to a college fund for Elisa instead of buying flowers for me?" Before I could answer him, he again reiterated, "Now I'm not giving up...don't think that I am 'cause I'm gonna fight it, and I'm gonna lick it and I'm gonna make it...I am going to live...but just in case..." His words trailed off.

I was stunned. Here was a young man who this day had just turned 16 years of age, and he was displaying more maturity and concern than most people develop in a long lifetime. I struggled for my composure, because so many times I had been told that he loved, and needed, to talk to me "more than anybody" because he could talk to me and I wouldn't cry. I could not cry...I did not cry...not on the outside where it would cause him additional distress, anyway.

As he watched me closely, I assured him that I would do everything in my power to carry out his wishes if that time came, which we both prayed it would not. We talked a long while that night about where we came from, why we are here and where we are going ultimately. Death had always been so difficult for me to discuss with anyone I loved…or anyone else for that matter. My sister-in-law had recently died after a long battle with cancer, and there were times that I knew she wanted to talk about her death that she knew was imminent, but I would always tell her she was going to get better…even though both of us knew better. I just couldn't face the fact of the reality, and because of that I had deprived her, and myself, of an honest conversation. And so I decided if Mike wanted to discuss his possible death, we would do just that.

We both felt that he WOULD make it because he was so strong, both in his mind and in his body. But we also both felt that if he didn't make it, then our Heavenly Father had a different plan for him…a special mission for him that, though we did not know or understand the plan at the present time, the time would come when we both would know and understand. And I think that at that place and time, both of us felt a sense of knowledge and understanding…and peace.

That night was largely sleepless for me because I realized without some visible directive from Mike, there was no way that I could do either of his two requests if that need presented itself. I prayed that I might know how to carry out his wishes. The next day, while we were playing scrabble, I got the idea of a "will."

Of course! If Mike would put his wishes in writing...in a sort of will, that would be the answer. We discussed the idea, and Mike worried that his parents would grieve if they thought he was writing out a will. So we decided he would write basically what he had requested of me...in his own words, we would fold it, put it in an envelope, put it between the pages of my Bible, and when the surgery was over and he was home again, he would retrieve the letter. Unless he chose to say something about it at some later date, that would be the end of it. Just he, his Uncle Garnet, and I would know it was available if needed. If, on the other hand, the need arose and it became necessary, then the letter would be read to his parents and to his doctor, and his instructions would be carried out. I explained to him that though I loved him dearly and would do all I could, that my hands were tied without his instructions, or will, in writing. He agreed, and it was not mentioned again for around six weeks until New Year's Eve...well, really New Year's Day, because it was some time after midnight on New Year's Day when Mike again called me into his room to talk.

Christmas 1985 was a happy time for us because Mike was feeling pretty well, the family was all together and his special nurse, Abby, was able to spend some time with us, too. New Year's Eve also was a special time. My husband and I spent the evening with the same group of friends that we had for more than 30 years, and Abby was able to spend the evening at our house with Mike where they could watch TV, play games, and eat the usual incredible edibles always around at the holidays. It was so wonderful to see Mike so happy, for that's truly the way he seemed. He had a confidence that was contagious, and we all had grown to love Abby. As most of her relatives were out of state, it made it especially nice for all of us to share some of the special times together.

Once again, as on his birthday night, when everyone had gone home and we were in fact on our way to bed, Mike once more wanted to talk. After we had gone into his room, he handed me a single sheet of white lined school notebook paper without saying a word. I looked at it and realized it was the "letter." He asked me to read it, check it for spelling or grammar errors, tell him if it was "all right," and then he would recopy it for me making any needed corrections. He watched intently as I read the letter…I could feel his eyes watching my face for any show of emotion and for my approval. The contents of the letter left me speechless…I was absolutely overwhelmed with admiration and respect, yes and love, for this young adult who sat opposite me waiting for my approval. "Is it all right, Aunt Jean?" I nodded mutely. "Are you sure?" "Oh yes, Mike, it is perfect." "Then I will go copy it," he replied, and as he took it, I could see his hand tremble…I never knew if it was from weakness or emotion. But I explained it did not need to be recopied…that it was fine. With that, he took it into the family room where he sat on a stool at the kitchen counter, and added diagonally across the bottom of the page these four words; "I Love You All, Mike." It was carefully folded, put into an envelope, sealed and placed into the Bible, as we had planned.

For the Love of Mike

Mike, age 2, enjoying his favorite Thanksgiving meal; mashed potatoes with chicken and noodles...and buttered corn etc., etc...

Mike, age 6...Little League had a positive thinker even then!

Pine Oak Minor League, 1978. Mike, front row left. Steve Cowan, Mike's dad is at rear row left.

For the Love of Mike

Mike, age 14... Kokomo
High School freshman...
1984.

The sports continue... "summer-
time, and the runnin' is easy."
And the winning is getting easier,
too...1984.

Kokomo High School track team...first time Regional Crown
Winners in KHS history! Champs displaying the trophy! Left
to right: Coach Ross Dwiggans, Carey Cox, Mike Cowan, Brent
Parrish, Tom Kirkmeyer, Pat Pollard, Tom Abney, Tony Manis,
Nick Moss, Jeff Dwiggans, Jim Keppler, Coach Ricke Stucker.
1984.

Mike (wearing the detested wig) with Aunt Jean taking a break from playing scrabble to sit on the front porch... Fall, 1985.

Mike and Elisa opening presents...Christmas 1985.

Mike in his room at Kokomo 'I did it before and I'll do it again'...showing off a small part of his ribbons and trophies just before leaving for Iowa. BMT

Almost brothers...Mike and Jeff Dwiggans. The snowball is being made for Elisa...

For the Love of Mike

Elisa and Mike boarding the plane for Iowa City and the BMT...January, 1986.

Memorial to Mike at Kokomo High School...

Dedication of memorial and Bradford Pear tree at Kokomo High School. Left to right: Coach Ross Dwiggans, Uncle Garnet Thornton, Aunt Jean, Chuck Jansen (first recipient of the Mike Cowan Memorial Scholarship Award and President of 1988 graduating class) and Chloie and Steve Cowan, Mike's parents...26 May, 1988.

Chapter Six

J anuary of 1986 came in with a fury all her own…cold, windy and lots of snow. Dr. Michael Trigg of the University of Wisconsin Hospital had been selected as Mike's surgeon because at that time, he had one of the highest success rates with bone marrow transplants of anyone in the United States (Dr. Trigg was running close to 22% success at that time). So it was with mixed emotions that Mike, his parents and I bundled into their car and headed north with great hope…and much fear of both the unknown as well as the known. Those numbers meant that of each 100 persons, who underwent transplants, 22 of them survived…and 78 of them did not survive! Mike would definitely be one of the 22!

Our trip to Wisconsin was a mixture of fear, but also of hope and excitement…and of fun. At the motel where we all stayed in the same room, it was so cold outside that we placed cokes outside the door for just a few minutes to get cold, and they instantly became partially frozen with slushy particles of ice. They tasted delicious. All four of us drank icy cokes and ate Better Cheddar crackers late into the night until we were stuffed. As we talked and laughed a lot, it was good...it was almost like the old days!

Once again, Mike had obtained literature detailing all the procedures of his impending transplant by one whom had survived it. After reading it, as he had done before, he wanted to make sure that his Mother and Dad not see it because he didn't want them to worry about the horror he would be facing. We were all very concerned because Mike had attained remission much slower than anticipated and we had the unspoken fear that he would not stay in remission. Nevertheless, driving down the snowy streets of Madison, Wisconsin, with snow piled at least five feet high on both sides of us, we were all determined to keep the all important positive attitude, and we found we would soon need it...particularly Mike.

"You know you're probably going to die, don't you?...that you will go through unbelievable experiences, and probably for nothing! These are the facts...are you aware of them? You think you have had it rough up to now...you don't know what rough is!" (Dear God, how can he speak like this! Does he know the Hell on earth this boy has gone through, the excruciating pain, the endless nausea...) The piercing dark eyes of the stocky doctor never wavered from the equally steady clear blue eyes of the tall, pale youth who faced him. Never breaking eye contact, Mike nodded his head mutely...then after a long pause that was electric, in a soft but firm voice he responded, "Not me, though. I'm gonna make it."

The doctor's right hand shot out and as he grasped Mike's hand in a firm handshake, he said, "You just might, Mike, you just might." Suddenly my intense dislike of the "heartless" doctor as he hurled the cruel (but honest) words at the sensitive youth turned to understanding...Mike had passed the test! At any sign of weakness, any doubt, any hesitation, his chances of a BMT would have been terminated instantly right there, right then! Dr. Trigg can only do a limited number of BMT's at a time and he must be selective. To be successful, coupled with a great deal of luck as well as skill, it demanded a total commitment on the part of both the doctor and the patient. What had appeared so heartless was, in fact, the most "heartfelt" thing that could have happened...it eliminated the weak before the BMT process began...from which there is no turning back. The most elemental Nature at work...survival of the fittest.

Upon returning to Indiana, Mike's energy levels fell lower and lower and our dreaded possibility became a reality. He was out of remission. Once again the rounds of chemotherapy and testing began, and this time a rather new and experimental (aren't they all?) drug was used and glory of glories, he was soon in remission again and ready to head to Dr. Trigg for the awaited BMT. A private pilot (arranged and paid for by the Kokomo Community Assistance Foundation, the wonderful organization that had set up a "Michael Cowan" fund to help throughout the monumental cost involved in Mike's illness) took Mike, his mother, and

For the Love of Mike

Elisa in his airplane. This eliminated the long and wearing car ride for Mike. (The awesome love and support of the community reaching out to the boy they had first admired for his winning spirit in sports now reached out still more for his spirit and courage as he was running his most important race of all...the race for his life. The people in Kokomo, Indiana and surrounding counties have hearts as big as the "Hoosier Heartland" where they live!)

At the airport, the reunion and love between Mike and Jeff, who loved each other like brothers, was one of the most touching scenes as they sat together quietly and seriously talking for the few minutes that they had. Both of them were fully aware of the seriousness of the ordeal ahead for Mike, because Jeff, too, was a confidant of Mike's and was well informed of any medical information that Mike knew. Jeff had quietly skipped school that morning without discussing it with anyone, including his father who was also his coach!

Once again, there were pictures to remember the occasion by, and then Mike, his mother, and Elisa were on their way to Iowa City, by plane, as Dr. Trigg had moved from the University of Wisconsin Hospital to the University of Iowa Hospital in Iowa City, Iowa. (Elisa would be the donor as they had been unsuccessful in locating a more nearly perfect match anywhere else.) I think, at that point we would have followed Dr. Trigg to "Timbuktu," if that were where he was. Mike's father would drive the family car to Iowa, and my husband and I would also drive our car.

Mike's great-uncle and aunt on his father's side, Charlene and Junior Shope, Abby and another nurse from Indianapolis, as well as several other relatives and friends also came to Iowa to visit Mike before his transplant began.

The hum of the small plane as it approached Iowa City, was probably the last quiet Mike and his family would know for several days. After quickly settling into the comfortable and spacious, nearly luxurious suite at the Ronald McDonald House, Mike got to meet all the athletes from both the Iowa basketball and football teams. The basketball players picked him up at the Ronald McDonald house and gave him both an Iowa State sweatshirt and sweater. Mike was wearing an Indiana University sweatshirt and cap at the time they picked him up, and took quite a ribbing...which he loved! They told him they would get him back in one piece, but they would make no promises about the "stuff" he was wearing!

The following day, the football team picked him up and took him with them to their practice...He loved every minute of both days, and everything was due to prior arrangements made by Kevin, the rowing coach from Purdue. Megan, the six-month-old baby girl of Kevin and Barb Sauer had been a patient in the Riley Pediatric Intensive Care Unit, which shared a common waiting room with the Teen Unit at Riley.

Kevin and Barb had met Mike and his family quite by accident—by destiny (?) at a restaurant close to Riley Hospital about three months into Mike's bout with leukemia. Kevin and Barb and their three healthy children, Nick, Kelly and baby Megan were eating at a nearby table when Nick asked with usual little boy candor and curiosity "Why doesn't he have any hair?"…pointing to Mike, as he walked over near to him, thoroughly assessing the situation.

The embarrassed parents never needed to answer. Quickly saying to them, "It's OK," Mike lovingly explained to the four or five year old Nick that he had gotten ill and to get "all well" again, he was taking medicine that caused his hair to just plain fall out! He also quickly assured the curious little boy and his family that it would grow back just like it had been before.

The young man enjoyed the tanned, healthy and happy young family…and the young couple felt compassion, and more, for the mature lad, little knowing that less than two weeks later their lives would be forever entangled. Their precious little Megan would be in the Intensive Care Unit, same hospital, same floor for six months until her little spirit finally returned to her Heavenly Father Who had lovingly loaned her for such a short time to the family who adored her.

In that six months period, the compassion grew to a mutual deep and abiding love as Mike and the family "adopted" each other…spending much of their days and nights together drawing strength each from the other. It was Mike, pale and ill, who made the decision that he would attend Megan's memorial services with his uncle and me. His trembling lips and hands were the only betrayal of the deep emotions he was feeling and the sympathy he felt for the friends who had become his extended family.

The funeral service for Megan was one of the most unusual, beautiful and awe inspiring services that any of the three of us had ever experienced. Following a fervent duet of the beautiful old hymn, Great is Thy Faithfulness, Kevin spoke and told of an event that happened just prior to their baby's death there in the Intensive Care Unit at Riley Hospital. With both his and his wife's permission, the following is an excerpt, verbatim, from a letter written recently by Kevin to me when I asked for his and Barbara's approval to include my recollections of that day in this book:

…After a torturous four month illness, her mother and I knew our little Megan Rose, 10 months old, was going to die. We had prayed for a miraculous healing, but her time was near.

"I was holding her in my arms and praying to Jesus to let her stay with us, but it was not to be. Megan became lifeless in my arms and we both cried uncontrollably. After holding her for a few minutes I felt an amazing peace and felt her weight being lifted from my arms. Through my tears, I looked and saw a bright light with arms outstretched taking Megan with Him. "Do you see it…do you see it?" Barb answered, "No—see what?" and all I could answer was "Jesus!" "The white light…it's Jesus, right here, taking Megan with Him." It was the most amazing experience of my life, to know without a doubt that our precious daughter was indeed in the arms of the Lord."

For the Love of Mike

There was complete silence, understanding and compassion as the devoted father and husband reverently and lovingly spoke of their all-encompassing faith to the packed church.

It was Kevin who assured Mike that he would attend college on the dreamed of athletic scholarship...that with his athletic ability, determination, character and super mental attitude, he could win a rowing scholarship to Purdue and live with them! How those plans (plus a trip to West Lafayette with Kevin to see a Purdue basketball game...seated right in the coaches section, no less) helped to erase the smells and pains of the hospital and replace it with enthusiasms and dreams...rivers and lakes...and boats and teammates... Life...beautiful, normal life! And while the plans and dreams were being formed, Kevin and Barb were introduced to the home made chicken and noodles that Mike would occasionally heat and serve as a midnight snack from the quart jars thawed and heated in the Teen Unit microwave! The shared Teen-Unit and Pediatric-Intensive-Care waiting room frequently became a place of shared plans and dreams for Mike, as the personable and optimistic young man also helped the young family to cope with their despairing hope for their precious baby girl.

Chapter Seven

*M*ike and Elisa both faced many grueling days of extensive tests before the actual BMT, during which they and their mother continued staying at the beautiful Ronald McDonald House. Here they became acquainted with many families facing the same ordeal, and fast and long-lasting friendships were once again newly established as many meals were prepared and shared.

It was here in the well-stocked kitchen that I had the space and resources to once again make the home made "chicken 'n noodles" not only for Mike, but also for his family and friends staying there. (At Mike's suggestion, I even filled a quart jar and took it to the hospital for Dr. Trigg to take home with him!) Mike wanted every one of his friends to enjoy the noodles with him, so many were required. They were a pleasure for me to make, rolling out the dough with the family size wooden rolling pin into several big pizza size circles on the more than ample, immaculate counters at the Ronald McDonald House. After drying a short time, each circle was rolled up and then hand cut on the cutting board with a sharp knife into the thin strips that were Mike's favorite shape for them. Of course, these prepared noodles were then dropped slowly into the seasoned boiling chicken broth and cooked until tender when they were combined with the succulent boiled chunks of chicken and served. Ummm...

During this time, my husband, Garnet, and I were staying in rooms graciously provided for us by the counseling service there at Iowa Hospital. The rooms, converted barracks from WW II, were very small, immaculate, and antiseptic with their white walls and old floors that were regularly scrubbed and polished. Each room was sparsely furnished with a vintage metal hospital bed of the '40's, and an equally small chest to hold one's necessities, but nevertheless, they were within walking distance of the hospital and Mike, and we were thankful for them. (Not only could we reach Mike shortly day or night, but also it gave us a great opportunity to walk. The wonderful exercise helped not only to relax our tense bodies, but also the brisk air cleared our lungs and minds to a degree.) It was here, also, that the outpatients stayed who were "county cases." All you needed to become a county case very quickly, if not immediately, was to acquire a terminal disease while uninsured! BMT alone can cost $100,000 and more! Much more!

And so it was here; as we sat in the common social room at night that once again we came face to face with raw courage. Having "cut" a record of two published original songs, which I had composed for my mother and father sometime before Mike's illness, it gave me great pleasure to give a record to any of the patients who cared to receive one. The songs were *"Prayer for Mother's Day"* and *"My Dad,"* and so they could be used as gifts for either or both of their parents for the approaching Mother's and Father's Day. Such small gifts could, and did, bring a sparkle of pleasure into many eyes.

In addition, inside the immense foyer at Iowa State Hospital, which in itself is awesome, being many stories high, sits a beautiful concert-sized grand piano. Open above the piano for several separate floors, each story protected by safety rails, there is room for patients or visitors to stand and listen to the beautiful tones as they rise all the way to the cathedral ceiling.

In addition to the artists who sometimes came and presented concerts, I was loaned a key to the locked piano and so could play it at my leisure…and that was sometime during every day or evening. What a privilege and pleasure it was for me to be able to go to that spot; to that piano, and while often surrounded by patients there, and always by those on different levels above me, to be able to play (or endeavor to play) their requests. If I weren't familiar with the song, quite often the patient would hum, sing or whistle the melody and we would improvise. This I had also done at Riley where there was an old battered upright piano in the combination recreation, class and cafeteria room. Badly scratched and abused, as the kids were free to play it whenever they chose, nevertheless the tone was beautiful and it was kept tuned. The joy that emanated around that old piano as we sang Christmas carols in July, and all of the songs, was the same as that around the beautiful, polished grand piano months later in Iowa.

Dwelling in the same unit as we did in Iowa was one particular young man whom I will call Jim, 37 years of age, a patient who was staying in the same building as we were while he awaited a spleen transplant. One evening he brought me a can of pop from his room (probably his last one), and asked if I would mind if he taped the music as I played the piano the next day. The hospital had loaned him a small cassette recorder as well as a blank tape for that purpose, and he wanted to tape the piano music so he could have it to listen to, following his surgery.

We didn't wait until the next day, because he did not know when he would get the call that the donor spleen was available...day or night. So it was that we walked that evening to the piano and I played his favorites... *"One Day At A Time," "Over The Rainbow," "Amazing Grace," "Theme from The Sting,"*...on and on until the tape was filled. He was so grateful, and I felt so blessed to be able to share something I loved just as much as he did...music. I had never met any of his family...I knew he was penniless, his clothes were pitifully shabby. I had never observed any visitors, but one thing had remained intact...his pride. And he had a record to give his "Mom" for Mother's Day...that was the extent of my knowledge of him.

A few days later, after the scheduled surgery that he

had told us about, I decided to visit him only to find he was not a registered patient. Next I checked the Intensive Care Unit…maybe he had encountered problems. Learning he was not there either, I went back to our "house." And there the sad news waited…he had not survived the surgery. The tears that I had always so carefully concealed from Mike engulfed me…sorrow, anger, hurt, frustration, helplessness, the unfairness of it all. Jim's needs were so simple, so elemental…just a bed, a few rags, a small amount of food for his body…and music for his soul.

A month later I received a letter from Jim's mother…my name and address was on the record he had so lovingly given her to keep for Mother's Day. She told me how he had listened to the tape constantly right up to the surgery (and I had heard it several times coming from his closed room, and more than once from the common recreation room where he and other patients gathered.) She closed by telling me that it was one of her most prized possessions…her link to the son she had loved and lost too soon. Like her son, she, too, was penniless from the financial strain and burdens of the long illness.

For the Love of Mike

Chapter Eight

*M*id-March in Iowa, as in Indiana, is often very windy and disagreeable, but on 13 March 1986, one year to the day since Mike had been diagnosed with leukemia, the sun was warm on our backs as we hurriedly walked the blocks to the University Hospital. The smell in the air of rich black soil promised springtime…of things soon bursting to life. The air at the hospital was equally optimistic. The carefree banter back and forth between Mike and Dr. Trigg carefully camouflaged the tension that was nearly palpable in the room. Mike appeared totally confident and unafraid…at that point he had total confidence that he would definitely be in the 22% who were successful. "Why not?" we had reasoned…he had everything on his side—youth, stamina, positive attitude, courage, the discipline and muscles of a trained athlete, fifteen years of nearly perfect health behind him…and the love and support and best wishes of his entire family and a whole city behind him as well (In addition, he had been riding a Schwinn combination rowing-bicycle machine in the exercise room there at the hospital to "get in shape.")

His home-town, Kokomo, had supported him 100% from the diagnosis of his illness: financially (via the "Mike Cowan Fund" set up by The Community Assistance Foundation through a local bank), emotionally (through cards and letters that numbered over 3000 to date!), scholastically (the coach had even brought his teammates and best friends out to Iowa to visit him), and newswise (The Kokomo Tribune had followed his progress every step of the way. As they had requested me to do, I called nearly every day, collect, to the Tribune staff writer, Christopher MacNeal, to report not only Mike's progress, but human-interest stories connected with his illness as well). In addition, local radio stations also covered his progress through interviews etc. From many of these articles and airings came the responses...letters and cards of encouragement, admiration, and inspiration.

On that fateful day that we had awaited, Elisa had been returned to her room...the two bags of precious, life-giving bone marrow, dark red and thick-looking, already having been extracted and waiting ready to enter Mike's body. Mike had just undergone three days of intensive chemotherapy and/or radiation that had totally destroyed every bit of his own bone marrow. Of course, in the process, he was left completely devoid of immunity to anything... something so simple as a common cold could prove fatal in such a condition. (How we take the wonderful miraculous machine we call the human body, for granted, as long as it is working perfectly! The awesome immune system that protects us like an all powerful army warding off any and all harmful enemy bacteria that would invade our body…able to discern, without fail, the "life-saving-ones" from the "life-taking-ones!")

Mike's infectious grin, as we walked into the room where he was receiving the bone marrow, suspended from an I.V. holder attached to his bed, warmed our hearts more than the warm sunshine we had recently left outside. "How are you feeling?" "Great!" came the answer. "No problems?" "No problems…that is except one…I sure could use a T-bone steak with a baked potato with lots of butter and sour cream…a salad…and some onion rings!" "Is it OK?", we asked Dr. Trigg, who was by his side. "You bet! And I could use some fresh, hot doughnuts!" (Doughnuts were Dr. Trigg's great passion and delight, and in the various cities that he flew into on his missions of mercy, he knew the locations of the bakeries that made the best doughnuts where he could "get 'em hot." Once when he had flown in from Washington, D.C., Mike and I got to sample one of them that came from a favorite bakery there!

How happy we all were to watch the hungry youth devour the large steak with all the trimmings…the entire meal. Then, with a mask over his nose and mouth, to walk across the hall to "cheer up" his sister, and to thank her for the gift of life, or at least a chance for it.

Elisa, in contrast to Mike was very pale and wan. In addition, she was quite sore. The ordeal of giving the bone marrow is much more uncomfortable for the donor than for the recipient. Also, it was extremely traumatic for this little strong-willed, but very dependent on her big brother, girl to undergo the emotional part of the transplant. Dr. Trigg had explained earlier that there is much mental stress on the donor who realizes that the very life of the recipient, in this case an adored only brother, depends totally on the acceptance or rejection of the bone marrow. And even though that is completely out of the control of the donor, still the guilt felt by that donor can be devastating.

Elisa was an extremely intelligent girl, and we had shared her joy when she was one of the first junior high students to be inducted into her school's National Honor Society. Still, she had the immaturity of a child, and the heart certainly rules the mind at that time in one's life. Of course, this also happens many more times than we might care to admit to those of us who have reached a degree of maturity. Nevertheless, as Mike entered the room, the eyes of these two met in total love and understanding...the tall blonde boy and his pretty thirteen year old brown-eyed, brunette sister, and all was well as the non-verbalized love flowed between the two.

Now the crucial hours began...the first 24, then 48, and then 72. Thank God, it was working, and working beautifully...perfectly. The "half match" of Elisa's bone marrow with Mike's was going without a hitch. Each day I phoned Christopher, the reporter at the Kokomo Tribune in Kokomo, Indiana, from the hospital in Iowa City, Iowa, with the wonderful reports. The same newspaper, whose sports writers so avidly followed all the sports at Kokomo High School, was now just as thoroughly covering each aspect of Mike's most difficult race of all...the race for his life through the life giving Bone Marrow Transplant.

The number of cards and letters that Mike received were mind-boggling. So many of them were from people who did not know him personally, but because he was such an inspiration to them to "keep on keeping on," they felt close to him. I could write another entire book just from the stories contained in those cards and letters of correspondence. From 8 to 80+ they wrote to him with one common thread...love, admiration and respect. And they brightened many long days for him...and for those of us who loved him. Cards filled the room, literally baskets full of cards plus those fastened to the walls of the room. Just to quote from one note from an elderly lady, who wrote these words, "My life had become empty and meaningless to me...nobody really cares about me. All I seemed to be was a burden. But since I have been reading each day of you and your courage, Mike, I've made up my mind to be grateful for each day...to quote you, 'one day at a time'."

We had heard from family members of some other patients of his that Dr. Trigg had developed, through research, the knowledge that by administering some particular drug he was able to prevent the horrible and feared condition where the body rejects its own skin. Not all of the patients were as fortunate as Mike in that aspect. The cries of the teen-age girl in the next room revealed her great pain as the nurses turned her, and the skin from her body was plastered by bits and pieces to the sheet on which she was lying. Her mother and I clung to each other in helpless pity outside her door in the hall, and I was so thankful that Mike had at least been spared that ordeal.

● ● ● ● ● ● ●

Why, in this book, do I tell these morbid stories? Why, indeed? Only because they are true, they happened, and so it must be told. It is only by being aware that we can care enough to do something about it. After spending 13 months almost daily in the midst of it with a loved one, complacency becomes impossible…unacceptable. These occurrences, terrible as they are, won't just "go away." There must be not just a cure for this horrible disease and others just as devastating, but the prevention. Leukemia and all the terrible diseases that destroy, second by second, literally are as terrifying as any medieval torture device ever designed. And they strike the helpless and most vulnerable among us.

All of those dedicated and caring doctors, nurses plus all the medical personnel who spent their days and nights then with Mike, and continue still today with their current patients fighting these very same nightmares, deserve more admiration, encouragement and support than I could ever express in mere words. Believe me, an incurable disease can happen to anybody…it can happen to you or me (or one you love) no matter how young, strong, or healthy you or your loved one might be. One day you have it all just like Mike...Youth, Health, Intelligence, Looks, Strength, Love...and the next you have lost all but the love...and the indomitable Will to survive.

For the Love of Mike

Chapter Nine

As the days passed, we were all so encouraged. Mike's energy level was increasing daily, and his appetite was excellent. To replace the massaging that my husband and I regularly did to the muscles in his calves as they cramped due to the inactivity they were unaccustomed to, once again he was able to exercise. (This brings to mind a time when we had to make a fast two-day trip back to Indiana about filing our taxes. Upon returning to his room, we could tell by the restlessness of his feet that he was having a difficult time with muscle spasms in his calf. As we quietly started rubbing his legs, he said, "Boy, am I glad to see you guys are back. I'll tell you one thing…when you get old and are in a nursing home, I'm gonna be the one that comes in and rubs your legs when they ache." Though we laughed about it many times later…by his standards, had he stopped to count, we would have been very old then, but to him we were just "ageless" and that's the best way to be. We have no doubts that if Mike had lived; he would have honored that promise if ever the need arose.) As Mike's strength increased, he could soon exercise for longer periods of time, on the Schwinn stationary bike that was there for the patients (or their caretakers). He was getting in shape to row on Kevin's Purdue rowing team!

The guarded Dr. Trigg told us the bone marrow was working...and we were guardedly ecstatic! Now if Mike could avoid any viral infections...Penicillin, any and all of the wonder drugs are totally impotent against any virus...they do not even slow it down. (A case in point is the common cold. If we take cold medicines, drink lots of fluids and get plenty of rest, the cold is usually gone in a week. On the other hand, eliminate the cold medicine, but abide by the other two and the cold usually lasts around seven days...our healthy immune systems get us well. Eliminate the immune system, and well, you see what I mean).

Perhaps the greatest danger following a bone marrow transplant is viral pneumonia, and the morning Mike began periodically coughing and was running a fever, our hearts were filled with fear. The culture was drawn and the doctor came into Mike's room where my husband and I were sitting with him while his parents and Elisa took a break at the local shopping mall. He asked that we call them immediately, as we needed to have a conference...Mike, his parents and us. His manner was very grave...the banter absent.

Chapter Ten

Y ou're not going to make it, Mike...we have nothing...
NOTHING...that will do a thing except perhaps slow
it, but that only slightly. You are going to die, Mike, I am
sorry." Time seemed to be repeating itself...even the words,
except now the words, "You know you're probably going to
die...even if you have the BMT?" had been altered to "you
are going to die," were the same as two and a half months
earlier.

No one can possibly comprehend the terror, the horror, the helplessness, the frustration, the anger, the denial,
and the all-enveloping pain of a time like that until one has
experienced it. This was even more hopelessly final than
the first day's diagnosis of cancer.

The response from the bed was a soft "no" as Mike's
eyes filled with tears...followed immediately by the glint of
fire in his eyes and his voice as he spat out, "Oh no, I'm
not...I am not going to die...I'm going to make it!" "Mike,
you must face the facts...you only have one chance in a
million..." Dr. Trigg never got to finish his sentence, as

Mike interceded, "ONE CHANCE...that's all I need..." and his index finger jabbed in the air toward the doctor to emphasize his point to him and then to each one of us in the room..."One chance...just give me one chance and I'll do it!

Once again the doctor's completely honest, and to all of us in that room both unacceptable and unbearable, words were uttered for a purpose. We had learned that Dr. Triggs' way to really deal fairly with a patient in that situation, particularly one as intelligent and decisive as Mike, was to be completely honest and open. Dr. Trigg went ahead to explain to Mike that if he would stay there in the room that had become "his own room," they could keep him more comfortable in the surroundings he was by now familiar with. Otherwise, he would be transferred to Pediatric Intensive Care Unit (PICU) where there is no day and no night...no rhythm, just the intense glare of a ceiling that is all white glaring fluorescent light. ICU...where tubes and monitors and IV's can be life saving servants of near miraculous proportions...or tortuous chambers of hissing "death prolongers." At best, all they could do was administer medications and treatments that were guaranteed almost 100% failures and Mike would soon have to be put on the ventilator.

Every bit of this was explained to Mike, and to all of us in just these same uncompromising words, but the decision was Mike's alone...he was going for that one chance in a million. My heart swelled with pride, and love (yes, and fear,) and great compassion at the raw courage and determination of the 16-year-old boy-man in that spacious card and silk flower filled room. None of us, including Mike, not one of us except the doctor had any idea or dreamed in our worst nightmares of the long and grueling hours that awaited Mike, and us, in the days ahead.

The staffs who work in every Pediatric ICU surely are among the most dedicated, caring and finest people whom I have ever known. One nurse in particular, Arnell Baughman, developed a special rapport with Mike in the time before the ventilator was hooked up. Once the ventilator is attached, all means of verbal communication from the patient is eliminated, and Mike's heart labored so hard…sustained 140-160 beats per minute…that he soon became too weak to write his messages to us. One afternoon, as I sat with him, I knew he was trying to communicate something to me.

Mike knew that each afternoon for some time I had played the concert grand piano located in the cathedral ceilinged atrium of the hospital. In fact, he was aware that I had quite a following who gathered in wheel chairs, came on crutches or came even though they were attached to various and assorted tubes…it made no difference, they still came for the music almost every day. One in particular, a four year old boy who had been very wary of me at the beginning and would maintain a safe 10 to 20 feet away from me in his miniature wheel chair, now often joined me where we would sing his favorite songs… *"Twinkle, Twinkle*

Little Star," or *"Jesus Loves Me,"* but his very favorite was *"Old McDonald Had A Farm (EE- I—, EE- I- OH!)"* His little chair now was as close as it could be without scratching the beautiful shiny ebony finish...he no longer associated me with the shots and pain he encountered, but with music and fun, and he sang with gusto!

There was always a mixture of parents or grandparents who would sometimes steal away from the rooms of their patients and quite often request the comforting old hymns they had learned to love in a more tranquil time of their lives. The patients on the various floors above me would call down their requests...the acoustics were so perfect that I heard them without difficulty. Of course, for some of the teens, the requested rock and roll and latest songs were not in my "repertoire" but I tried and it was always a special time for all of us, I believe.

One day, two young men were cleaning the beautiful chandeliers and light fixtures in the area and wanted to hear *"The Sting"*...and wildly applauded my less than professional efforts. Probably the overall favorite of everybody seemed to be *"Somewhere Over The Rainbow,"* including Mike and the nurses..."somewhere over the rainbow skies are blue, and the dreams that you dare to dream really do come true." In that massive and elegant surrounding, mostly the audience were all simple folks whose love of music took them away, for a few moments, from the antiseptic halls and I.V.'s to happier times, the memories of sunshine...and flowers... and green grass beside streams or ponds…and carefree times. Or maybe the peace to accept the things they could not change. "Dear God, grant unto me the serenity…grant Mike…to accept the things I cannot change, the courage to change the things I can, and the wisdom to know the difference…"

Mike wrote…scrawled…the single word "piano" on the pad I held toward him, as I could not understand the message he was trying to give me. "You want me to go play the piano?" His thumb and third finger formed the circle as he gave me the "OK" sign. A smile flickered on his face briefly. "I will, all your favorites, then I'll be back and tell you all about it and who was there." He had heard in detail about the four-year-old *"Old Macdonald had a Farm"* boy as well as all the others.

For the Love of Mike

Chapter Eleven

*T*he days dragged by. By now, Mike was receiving medication that rendered him totally helpless...unable to move. The same medicine, one of the physicians explained, that is used to tranquilize animals from airplanes in the wilds, where dart guns are used to administer the tranquilizer shots to the creatures. The animals, though aware, are thus rendered utterly motionless...paralyzed...only their eyes frantic movements betraying their fear until their glorious freedom is again restored to them.

Of all the ordeals of the past, this had to be the worst. All of the feelings, the comprehension, the awareness, are all intact, but combined with complete and total immobility...total paralysis. Not to be able to even scratch his nose if it tickled or itched, (and it had so often throughout his illness from the medications etc.) or to tell of the muscle spasms that periodically caused the "charley-horses" to hit in the calves or thighs of his athletic legs. Nor even to be able to communicate it so we could help him as we had in the past. The only sounds the hissing, clicking, fizzing, thumping noises of the endless machines. I could hardly stand to leave him at all...I knew he knew when I walked in to the room, because all of his vital signs told us. His pulse rate decreased. I talked to him, as nearly as I could, non-stop. "It's Monday morning, Mike...seven o'clock, and as your Uncle Garnet and I walked over, we saw our first robin. Your mom and dad will be over shortly. It's not quite as warm today. The team was out practicing...I saw the guy who talked to you about your I.U. sweatshirt...Does your nose itch? I'm going to rub your feet and legs for you...We won't leave you...I'm right here...I love you...we love you...we won't leave you, I promise...I promise."

Chapter Twelve

Florida on the Dock, 14 February, 1991...

*A*rnell, the wonderful friend and nurse who stayed with him when one of the family wasn't there, kept up the same talk with him. She had heard me read Mike the 23rd Psalm one day, and as I came back later and stepped into his room, I saw her holding his motionless hand and praying with him for strength and peace.

Many had come from Indiana to visit Mike over the three weeks. Among them were his coach and two of the track team who were best friends...Jeff, who hadn't seen him since the day he flew out from Kokomo, and Tom. This was while Mike was on the ventilator, but before he had received the paralyzing medication. He was so determined to use his will to "cooperate" with the ventilator (to allow the ventilator to breathe for him, an almost impossible feat at best.) He did so for a short time, and so it was that though he could not respond verbally, due to the tube that was down his throat, he could hear them and acknowledge them by nodding his head or the familiar "thumbs up." Their young voices filled with hope as they tried to encourage him, "Mike, we're gonna go run around the campus...this run's for you...you're gonna make it, Mike...we're really going to hit it hard and fast out there for you, Mike..." They, nor we, could understand why and how this could happen to Mike, but as they stood by his bed the last time, I'm sure they all knew, we all knew...that would be the final time.

The days passed. How long could the strong heart keep beating its staccato pace? The life support was prolonging the torture. Some of us were sitting beside him around the clock except when Arnell was there. One day my daughter, Linda Foster, whom Mike loved and respected, had driven over from Indiana to be with him. She told us later as she sat beside his immobilized body and watched the struggle, the brave but hopeless struggle going on, she held his hand and talked to him. She told him how hard and fearlessly he had fought...how proud we all were of him, how much we all loved him and that it was all right for him to stop fighting and rest...that not one of us would ever think he had not given his best in the fight.

This was the possibility that Mike had discussed with me all those eons ago...(could it possibly only be five months?),...when he had called me to his room on his birthday, and thanked me for "the best birthday of my life in some ways, but it could be my last one," and this said as tears brimmed his beautiful young eyes. We both felt that if, in spite of all his efforts, he did not make it, then his Heavenly Father must have felt he had completed his mission on this earth (and what a noble mission as he touched, and inspired literally thousands of lives through personal contact, as well as the newspaper coverage.) And perhaps even more importantly, another mission awaited him as he "graduated" from this earthly existence to the next level of his existence. And as we talked on that November night, neither of us doubted that there would indeed be that next level for all of us.

As Linda spoke the words to him that it was all right...whatever he decided...that he would certainly have given his very best and most inspired effort to this biggest race of all, she sensed a feeling of peace emanate from Mike...

The doctor was discussing with Mike's parents, with all of us, the fact that nothing was helping Mike. He said that Mike's one in a million chance had expired also...that there was no activity in the brain, that legally he was "brain dead." The parents agonized "no" barely audible, still filled the room...all that was sustaining his life was the life supports that were attached to him. We knew that the purring, hissing, thumping, whistling noises were all that was between Mike's tortured and immobilized body on the narrow hospital bed and his spirit soaring free to that "great beyond."

I knew that the unbelievable, the unthinkable, the

unbearable had happened. The time had come that I must follow Mike's wishes, and I told all of them that Mike had also prepared for this possibility…about the letter which he had written and given to me on New Year's Day Eve, and wanted me to read to all of them. It had been brought to Iowa with the belief and prayer that it would never need to be read, but returned to Mike, unopened, at a later time. Mutely, they nodded to me and I read the letter that had been sealed until that moment:

"To my loved ones,

"I know if you guys get this letter it's going to be a very hard time for you. But remember you all have been through a lot in your lives and this will be another thing you all can get through. I know it doesn't seem fair but remember you all still have each other and that's more than a lot of people have. I know its going to take time but if you all keep a good attitude and work together, everything will be okay. I don't want anyone to feel sorry for me because remember I'm in the Lord's hands now and that is the best place to be. Since this has happened, there are a few things I want done.

1) "I would like to see half of the memorials go toward Elisa's schooling. She deserves all the help she can get considering all the hard work she puts forth for school.

2) "I hope Aunt Jean won't have to give you this letter for this one, but if I'm on the life support system and there is no hope, I would like to be taken off of it. I don't

want any of you to feel bad about this decision because that was the way I wanted it. Remember, if it comes down to this you're doing the best thing for me.

3) "From this day on, I would like you to remember me as one who took it one day at a time even though during my time with leukemia things were up and down. I always tried to keep a good attitude and that one thing helped me get through the first few months and the time after I relapsed. I know I had some good moments in sports, but I just want to be remembered as one who tried and fought his best to beat cancer and darn near did it. If any of you come down with an illness, please don't ever give up because there is always hope and with faith in God and a good attitude, that will make your chances better. This is the way I approached my illness and I was around quite awhile. I know there will be days you'll feel like quitting if you come down with an illness because I had days like this. But those are the days you have to talk to someone and think of your family and friends and you can always count on the Lord to be there for you. So I'm saying don't ever give up because that's not the to way to handle anything.

"I

"Love

"You

"All,

Mike"

As the last words of the letter were read, Dr. Trigg took charge and said that Mike in his wisdom had removed the decision from all of us...that perhaps we would want to wait there in the consultation room until it was all over. I knew there was no way I would wait in that consultation room...though I felt I could not be in the room as the life support was removed, I knew I could not, I would not, be anywhere but with Mike when that happened. His biggest fear had been in being alone. "We will never leave you alone...don't worry." How many times had these words been spoken through the long months at Riley Hospital in Indianapolis, at Wisconsin Medical Center where we had initially met Dr. Trigg and finally at Iowa University Hospital where Mike's inert body now lay.

According to the doctors and all of the information from the various monitors, at this point Mike had no cognizance at all; he would have no knowledge or ability to know whether he was alone or if the room was filled with people. Maybe he would not know, but it made no difference...the promise had been made and would be honored. And so it was that as his hand was held in deepest love while our collective hearts were breaking, the tubes were all removed from Mike's body, and the room was silent..

Always in my mind, as I had seen in movies, this act of disconnection would be followed by a peaceful sleep from which there would be no awakening. How heart breakingly different that assumption was from the reality! As the paralyzing medication that was keeping his body immobilized was discontinued and consciousness returned, the physical strong athletic fighter reaction took over, and the last and final great struggle began.

Elisa's keening cry of anguish filled the room, "Mike, you can't die, you can't, you can't...you promised me...you can't die...you can't die..." and as she sobbed uncontrollably, Dr. Trigg who was standing beside Mike and had until that moment maintained complete composure and been motionless, turned away and his broken sob of anguish joined Elisa's...and ours. It hit me then more than at any other time that the doctor who devoted all of his time and energy, and yes, brilliant intellectual ability to prevent this finale had also lost...a patient, but more importantly one of his "kids"...a boy whom he had come to know, respect and to love. And I felt love and compassion for him...and understanding.

Across the bed from Elisa and me, beside the doctor was the faithful Arnell, the young nurse who had so faithfully given Mike the moral support he needed...the one who read to him, talked to him...and prayed with him. Mike's Uncle Garnet and his parents were standing mutely at the foot of the bed, where his parents were holding each other in mutual support.

For the Love of Mike

Chapter Thirteen

Florida on the Dock...19 February 1992

*I*t has taken a year to deal with the anguish of that moment in 1986...to return to writing this story. And yet, I know that was not the end for Mike...but only a beautiful beginning. I remember again the words that passed between us on his 16th birthday as he discussed with me to please not permit the life support to go on endlessly...and to realize that the decision was his. But oh, the agony of going through that ordeal with a loved one!

Mike's funeral service at the Main Street Christian Church in Kokomo, where he and his family were members and had been supported both spiritually and financially throughout his ordeal by the entire congregation, was packed to standing room only with all who had followed his illness so faithfully. One could have heard a pin drop as for part of his memorial service, I read his letter that was addressed "to my loved ones" to all of his school friends, fellow athletes, school teachers, relatives and all who were assembled there in that packed building. There was total and reverent silence until his last line, "I love you all," and then the heartbreak of all the young friends in that room could be suppressed no longer.

Chapter Fourteen

Florida on the dock, February 1993...

*A*s time passes by, the pain somehow, though not truly subsiding, becomes less acute...even though the memories and notes still remain as fresh as yesterday...Truly Mike's mission, in person, here on this earth had ended, but the influence, the inspiration brought about in 16 short years live on...and on...

Late Fall—1997—Conclusion

The year that Mike would have graduated from Kokomo High School, 1988, all of his family were invited to the Graduation Ceremony. There was an empty chair which held a single long stemmed red rose, like the other graduates were carrying, for Mike, and certainly he was there in spirit as his teachers, coach, principal and all his classmates honored and paid tribute to him. The award for good sportsmanship and mental attitude was renamed "The Michael

Cowan Mental Attitude Award" in his honor. Presently, in addition to the mental attitude award that is presented every fall, another award, the "Mike Cowan Memorial Scholarship" is awarded each spring at graduation. Charles "Chuck" Jansen, another teammate and close friend, was the first recipient of this award in 1988. This is awarded for scholarship achievement to a boy or girl who has also earned a letter in some sport during his or her high school attendance. In addition to the honor, it also includes a cash amount which has been earned throughout the entire school year by all of the members of the "K" Club, athletes who have earned their letter in sports.

As Ross Dwiggins, Mike's coach and the father of one of his dearest friends, Jeff, in his words to encourage me to complete and publish this book recently told me, "Mike Cowan is not forgotten by Kokomo High School. His achievements in cross country running, his ability to inspire his teammates, and his wonderful attitude in every endeavor he undertook, including his last and biggest race of all against leukemia, will long be remembered."

In the fall of 1997 Jeff learned that I was going to hopefully finish, as well as publish, the book that has been in the developmental stage for so many years. He sent me a letter, via e-mail, of remembrance and tribute to Mike, the friend he viewed as a brother. As I edit this manuscript for publishing, I would like to insert, verbatim, his account of many special days and events. The selected portions are too touching to do otherwise. Although I realize there will be some repetition, it is from a teammate whose descriptions impart a whole new perspective of the same events. With Jeff's permission, the following excerpts are in his own words:

"My earliest recollection of Mike Cowan was in the late fall of 1983. I was a freshman at Haworth High School and Mike was an eighth grader at Lafayette Park Middle School. It was during this time that Mike started jumping in a few local Club Kokomo road races. Club Kokomo was a local organization that sponsored a lot of athletic events, running road races really, for local athletes. I started seeing Mike at these events and had heard that he was a good runner from other runners in the area.

"In the spring of 1984 it became apparent that two local high schools would be combined, Kokomo High School and Haworth High School. I was very excited about that because all of my running rivals like Carey Cox, Mike, and Tom Kirkmeyer would be teammates instead of "enemies." I saw Mike at a few more Club Kokomo events in the spring of 1984 and we actually exchanged some friendly words. The one thing I immediately noticed about Mike was that he was always supremely confident and in a good mood.

"In May of 1984 I began toying with the idea of running the Indy 500 Mini Marathon in Indianapolis. This was something I wasn't too sure about since the race itself was 13.1 miles and I had never even run 10 miles in practice before. My parents said it would be O.K. to run but because my father was teaching school and race was on a Friday I would need to find a ride. I called Club Kokomo

Secretary Mark Shorter and he said he would be glad to take me. He also said another runner would be traveling with us. "Who's that," I said. "It's Mike Cowan," he exclaimed. Hmmm, I thought to myself. Mike had been getting increasingly closer to beating me in some of these road races. I wonder if we'll get along. Then Mr. Shorter reminded me that it would be a good idea to train for this race and suggested he, Mike, and I get together at Highland Park in Kokomo to do some long training runs. "Sure," I said.

"Mike and I met Mr. Shorter at Highland Park for one training run that I can remember. We didn't say a whole lot to each other as both of us were probably trying to prove something to the other. I came away from my first "formal" meeting with Mike feeling pretty good about him. He seemed very likable, laughed a lot, joked around, and made the hard work seem like fun. I couldn't help but liking him...

"On May 25, 1984, Mike and I jumped in the car with Mark Shorter very early in the morning and drove to Indianapolis. We got to the event and began to warm up. I was very nervous and something inside me was really questioning whether I could finish this 13.1-mile race...

"Mike was so loose before the start of the race. He was joking about how we were going to need a lift from one of the race cars when we finally made it to the Motor Speedway at the 12th mile. It was a mass of humanity at the starting line. There were 3,500 runners. The gunshot rang out and we were off. I was surprised about how good I felt once we got going and how fresh my legs felt. I lost sight of Mike, however, and so I decided to pace off Mr. Shorter.

"Finally, about 3-4 miles into the race I saw Mike up ahead of me. I came up along side of him. What a miracle to find Mike, I thought, in this sea of humanity. When I caught Mike he wasn't breathing hard at all. He was laughing about how he got too excited and went out too fast. He said, "Why don't we run this thing together? I can draft off of you and you can draft off of me so we won't both have to always run dead into the wind." "Sounds good to me" I said, still wondering if I could even finish a 13.1 mile race.

"The next eight miles would be the most incredible of my life. We talked about everything in those next 50 minutes...girlfriends, school, life, running, friends, everything. We did everything but concentrate on the race. At eight miles I told Mike I would have to slow down. I was getting a cramp. Mike encouraged me not to give up or give in. He told me to just scream out loud and the cramp would eventually go away. So I did. I scared a few people, but the cramp went away. Then at 10 miles, Mike said that he needed to slow down. I took my turn encouraging him. "We've come too far already," I said. I slowed down a bit for Mike since he had slowed down for me.

At 11 miles we were back in business, targeting various runners that we wanted to pass. We had done this the whole race, making small surges to pass groups of people. We were both surprised at how well we were doing.

"Just before the 12 mile mark, Mike told me to run

ahead of him. "You have to go this time," he said. "Don't worry about me." He explained that this time he really was out of gas. It was either slow down or not finish. I reluctantly went ahead. I entered the Motor Speedway and crossed the line in 1 hour and 27 minutes and 53 seconds. I was exhausted but thrilled. I started looking immediately for Mike. Mike came barreling down the track and across the finish line in 1 hour 28 minutes and 50 seconds, passing three more people in the last few meters and finishing less than a minute behind me. We had just finished 250th and 314th out of what would turn out to be officially more than 4000 finishers. (Bold Italics added) We were ecstatic. We hugged each other at the finish. A friendship was truly born. We could not stop talking for weeks about neither one of us could have done it without the other. I might add, though, that it was Mike, not me who really initiated this encouragement. He truly was an especially strong person.

"I will never forget that day and I will never forget the part that Mike played in it. It was a special moment that for me is forever suspended in time. My words do not adequately describe or explain the hows and whys of the way that bond was formed that day. I can only say that I guess God did it to bring Him glory.

"Mike and I continued our friendship that summer spending the night at each other's houses, going on double dates, running together, talking on the phone about our future and how we would both like to compete in the state cross country meet someday. Our friendship became more solidified and we were almost like brothers.

"School started and I was a sophomore at KHS and Mike was a freshman. Mike and I traded places beating each other back and forth in meets. I don't think it put a strain on things...the competition and all...we both had so much respect for the other, we felt competition was good and would make us both better. Mike set the freshman school record for a 5K with a time of 17.59 in a meet on September 6, 1984 and would later lower that to 16.55. Mike and I nailed down 19th and 22nd place respectively in the Logansport Regional on October 20th to help Kokomo finish first, a team goal we had both set for ourselves at the beginning of the year...

The indoor track season started around January/February of 1985. Mike and I began training indoors to get ready. Everything seemed to be according to plan. Mike and I were both fit and leading the way in practices. Then, totally out of the blue, Mike got to where he was unusually tired and had trouble finishing workouts. This was very, very unlike Mike. He was always a warrior in workouts and meets. He never quit right in the middle of a workout. Mike confided in me that he was throwing up at home and always felt like sleeping. I told him that sounded serious and he should see a doctor, but Mike felt that he probably had a nagging case of the flu. Mike's problems in practice didn't go away. I watched Mike have absolutely terrible practices for a whole week. I couldn't understand it. I questioned whether Mike had lived up to his end of the bargain by practicing all winter. He assured me he had. It just looked like he was totally out of shape.

Finally, after about 7-10 days of this, we were running laps indoors when Mike just stopped and went over to a trashcan and threw up. I walked over to the stairwell and found Mike sitting on the stairs with his face buried in his hands and crying. I said "Mike, you gotta promise me that you are going to see a doctor. This is not normal. You are sick." Mike told me that the appointment was already made. I felt relieved and told him to just go home. I went over and told the coach that Mike was going home ill."

Jeff continued in his letter to tell of his and the teams running past the hospital to see Mike the day of his diagnosis with leukemia, the utter shock and disbelief of all the teammates at the news, about them all hugging Mike, hearing the details of the road ahead for Mike from the doctor: "chemotherapy, missed school, no athletics, a possible bone marrow transplant if nothing else worked. I could not believe it. Soon it was Mike encouraging all of us friends not to worry. I distinctly remember Mike saying that he would beat this disease. We were all more stressed out than Mike. Mike became the calmest person in the room while everyone else tried to get a grip on things. His attitude was amazingly positive. I apologized to Mike for questioning his drive and determination when he wasn't finishing his workouts. If I had only known. Mike forgave me without hesitation and told me to go out and have a good season."

For the Love of Mike

"Over the next year I went to see Mike several times in the hospital during his chemotherapy treatments. His sister, Elisa, was always there along with the rest of Mike's family. I know it was really hard on them. I always found Mike in good spirits. He even made fun of himself when he lost his hair during chemo. He always talked about getting well, continuing training, and doing stuff with the guys. I admired Mike's courage...I wondered how I would do in Mike's shoes. Not very well, I concluded.

Occasionally, Mike's condition fell into remission, and he actually got to come home during these brief times. We played cards, video games, caught up on the girlfriend scene, talked about running, and stayed over at each other's house a few times. It was so good to have Mike in town. Mike even went out jogging a few times to my disbelief. He seemed invincible. Whatever blow life dealt him, he just fought back.

Mike began dropping hints every now and then that he was a born again Christian. I would often ask Mike where he got all of his courage and strength from. I think it made me feel more comfortable to ask questions like that because the reality of the situation was so intense. Mike had given vague answers before, but over the last few months of his life I started hearing him talk about God a lot more. I didn't understand it at first. I saw a minister in Mike's room a few times during my hospital visits and I also saw a Bible on Mike's table in the hospital room. We didn't talk about it too much, but Mike was clearly becoming more religious to me. In 1988 I became a Christian and it was Mike's example that the Lord had brought back to memory. In fact, Mike's death was a stumbling block to me becoming a Christian for awhile. I couldn't understand why God would take him away at such a young age. *Eventually, however, I came to the conclusion that although I didn't understand it, God had bigger plans for Mike in death than in life.* (Italics added) Mike would not want my lack of understanding of his death to keep me out of heaven. I decided it was best to join Mike in faith toward God and He'll explain it to both of us sometime down the road...

I thought I would share this funny story about Mike. During one of his remission periods in the summer of 1985, Mike and I went to Kings Island in Ohio, a big amusement park. Mike had his wig on at the time. We got on a big roller coaster called the Racer. During the ride on one hill, Mike's wig flew off of his head and down to the ground. We both laughed our heads off. The girls sitting behind us couldn't figure what was going on. Mike proceeded to tell me how much he hated that wig when I suggested we get a park supervisor to fetch his wig from under the coaster. So we left the wig at Kings Island and had a good laugh. Mike vowed not to wear another wig, but I think he eventually did briefly—I can't remember for sure...

"I knew that Mike had just had a bone marrow transplant on March 14, 1986. I had seen him off at the airport along with Elisa and his mom...I have always appreciated the love that Elisa showed by contributing the bone marrow...

For the Love of Mike

"I was playing a soccer match in the Police Athletic League in March of 1986 when a long time friend of mine pulled me to the side to tell me that Mike was dying at the University of Iowa Hospital in Iowa City and that one of his last few requests was to see me…I thought things had gone well. I even talked to Mike on the phone and he assured me "I'm coming home soon." I had no idea things would turn for the worse. I ran home as fast as I could leaving the game in progress and I flew to Iowa City for the weekend and spent several hours in Mike's intensive care facility. He looked much different than before with all kinds of tubes connected to him, monitors, nurses constantly coming and going, etc. I found myself actually praying for the suffering to stop. I said "Please, God, heal Mike completely and get him out of here or let him go in peace. Please take away the pain." I didn't know what to do. I got to hold Mike's hand and speak a few words of encouragement to him. And yes, one last time, even in all this pain, I got to see Mike Cowan smile. With death itself pounding on his doors, Mike Cowan could still smile.

"I've never met anyone like Mike. When I left Iowa City, things looked grim. I knew that might be the last time I would see Mike. But I had hope. Mike had given me that hope…

"Mike had written me a letter on March 5, 1986, from Iowa City. I still keep it in a special place. I think in his own words Mike sums up what he was all about. He says in the letter, *try not to get down on yourself so much. Just tell yourself that next time (you run) you can do it and you will. Jeff, the best way to handle it is to take it one day at a time. Just worry about it for the rest of that day and think about what went wrong and what to do next time you're in that situation. I hope you don't have a bad race this year, but if it happens just remember to keep your head up because that will make you even more of a winner."* (Italics added)

"…I remember running that '86 season in track. On many an occasion, I felt like Mike was running right beside me like he did in Indianapolis. I could hear Mike pushing me along and encouraging me…still have all the articles from the Kokomo Tribune that told Mike's story, ..the school newspaper, the poems written by classmates, a few pictures…

"Mike is still an inspiration to me today. The letter he wrote to family and friends about "not giving up, having hope and faith in God, and keeping a good attitude" will always stick with me…I look forward to the day that I can be reunited with Mike and we can run along the streets of gold…Mike won the only race that really counts—the eternal race. He was a great friend and even a brother to me…For just a second, I can close my eyes and I see Mike running next to me through the streets of Indianapolis. *"Why don't we run this thing together, Jeff?!"* *"Sure, Mike, let's run this thing together."*

Chapter Fifteen

T he following spring after the graduation of Mike's class, at the front entrance to the high school, just to the right of the walk, the athletic department planted a memorial Bradford pear tree, in front of which was a gray stone monument presented by the entire Kokomo High School. Engraved on the stone are these words copied from Mike's letter, "DON'T EVER GIVE UP" plus his name and the date of his birth and death. On either side of the monument and tree, were classroom constructed wooden benches where the students or staff might sit and talk, or read the words etched there…and ponder them…

Each springtime, at Memorial Day, my husband, Mike's uncle, always helped me decorate the memorial area with bright colored silk flowers, which added to the pleasant area for those who regularly gather there. At Christmas, also, around the area was decorated with red and white silk poinsettias and other Christmas greenery, in remembrance of the boy who loved life so passionately and lived it to the fullest…who touched more lives in 16 short years than most of us could in 16 lifetimes.

The past tense has been used in describing the beautiful memorial area, because within the last several months Kokomo High School has begun adding extensive additions to, as well as remodeling, the present school structure. In so doing, the living memorial Bradford Pear tree was lost, and the other pieces were put into safe storage until completion of the remodeling. The 1988 graduating class, of which Mike would have been a member, has for their tenth year reunion project for the spring of 1998, taken upon themselves to restore the complete Mike Cowan Memorial area, including planting another tree, and then once again we will be able to keep flowers there in remembrance of Mike. The publication date of this memorial book is also scheduled for that time.

Mike will never be forgotten by those of us who loved him… and now, maybe by many of you who never knew him except through this book written in remembrance *"For the Love of Mike."*

• • • • • • • •

"From this day on, I would like you to remember me as someone who took it one day at a time. Even though during my time with leukemia things were up and down, I always tried to keep a good attitude and that one thing helped me get through the first few months and the time after I relapsed. I know I had some good moments in sports, but I just want to be remembered as one who tried and fought his best to beat cancer and darn near did it. If any of you come down with an illness, please don't ever give up because there is always hope and with faith in God and a good attitude, that will make your chances better. This is the way I approached my illness and I was around quite awhile. I know there will be days you'll feel like quitting if you come down with an illness because I had days like this. But those are the days you have to talk to someone and think of your family and friends and you can always count on the Lord to be there for you. *So I'm saying don't ever give up because that's not the way to handle anything."*

"I...Love...You...All..., Mike"

(Last paragraph of a letter written by
Michael Scott Cowan, 2 January 1986, age 16 years)
Italics added.

In Memory of Mike

It's been a year since that sad day we had
to say good-bye
>*To one whose life was like a ray of*
>*sunshine in our sky.*

So good, so young, so positive in every
race he faced...
>*So disciplined, so kind, so loved...so truly*
>*"full of grace."*

He wrote a letter to us, all, to keep on
"keeping on"...
>*Of how he'd fought the cancer hard and*
>*quoting, "darn near won."*

He wouldn't want us grieving now in futile,
helpless tears,
>*But out there giving life our best as days*
>*roll into years.*

We won't forget you, ever, Mike...you're
with us all the way...
>*Inspiring us, reminding us, to give*
>*our best EACH day.*

>*—written by Aunt Jean...1987*

...For unto whomsoever much is given, of him shall be much required..."

From the gospel of St. Luke, 13:48

Epilogue

1997

This book has been written in installments over a period of nine years...and always in the same location, on a dock at Clearwater Beach, Florida, and always on the same dog-eared yellow legal pad...February, 1988, '89, '90, '91, '92, and '93, and completed in 1997. The reason for inserting the dates and locations were because this was such a highly charged emotional undertaking for me that it has taken that long, and it seemed that those of you who read this were entitled to know that. To protect their privacy, the names of all the patients and hospital personnel were changed and are fictitious with the exception of the physicians and the ICU nurse who was with Mike the last weeks of his life. The names of the coaches, school personnel, personal friends and teammates were not changed, as well as Kevin Sauer, the rowing coach from Purdue University, and his family. In addition, all family members' names are also correct.

For the Love of Mike

I wish that Mike could have written this, as we both planned, with another ending, but this isn't a novel, this is life…just as it happened. I feel very blessed to have been close enough to him to write these pages "For the Love of Mike." I hope they will inspire the reader with his courage and love as he inspired those of us who lived this time with him.

The Answer

"We ask for strength, and God gives us difficulties,

which makes strength…

"We pray for wisdom, and God sends problems,

the solution of which develops wisdom…

"We plead for prosperity, and God gives us brains

and brawn to work…

"We plead for courage, and God gives us

dangers to overcome…

"We ask for favors, and God gives us opportunities…

This is the answer!"

—Author unknown

Order Form

For the Love of Mike

To order: *Shadybrook Publishing*
c/o 1429 Chase Court
Carmel, Indiana 46032
Phone: 317-844-8622

Ship to:

*Name*_____

*Address*_____

*City*_____

*State*_____ *Zip*_____

*Telephone*_____

Please send:

_____*book(s) at $14.95* $_____

Sales tax (Indiana residents add $.90 per book) $_____

Shipping and handling (Add $3.00 for first book, $_____
$.75 per additional book)

TOTAL $_____

Quantity discounts available. Call for information.
Method of payment: check or money order accepted.

For the Love of Mike